Pig Pens

Pam Scheunem[...]

Illustrated by C.A. [...]

Consulting Editor, Diane Craig, M.A./Reading Specialist

ABDO
Publishing Company

Published by ABDO Publishing Company, 4940 Viking Drive, Edina, Minnesota 55435.

Printed in the United States.

Credits
Edited by: Pam Price
Curriculum Coordinator: Nancy Tuminelly
Cover and Interior Design and Production: Mighty Media
Photo Credits: Brand X Pictures, Kelly Doudna, Image Source, ShutterStock

Library of Congress Cataloging-in-Publication Data

Scheunemann, Pam, 1955-
    Pig pens / Pam Scheunemann ; illustrated by C.A. Nobens.
        p. cm. -- (Fact & fiction. Animal tales)
    Includes index.
    Summary: Riblet and his brothers and sister participate in the Wallow School Fun Run to win a very special prize. Contains facts about pigs.
    ISBN 1-59679-959-5 (hardcover)
    ISBN 1-59679-960-9 (paperback)
    [1. Pigs--Fiction. 2. Contests--Fiction.] I. Nobens, C.A., ill. II. Title. III. Series.

PZ7.S34424Pig 2006
[E]--dc22

                                                                                    2005024444

SandCastle Level: Fluent

SandCastle™ books are created by a professional team of educators, reading specialists, and content developers around five essential components—phonemic awareness, phonics, vocabulary, text comprehension, and fluency—to assist young readers as they develop reading skills and strategies and increase their general knowledge. All books are written, reviewed, and levels for guided reading, early reading intervention, and Accelerated Reader® programs for use in shared, guided, and independent reading and writing activities to support a balanced approach to literacy instruction. The SandCastle™ series has four levels that correspond to early literacy development. The levels help teachers and parents select appropriate books for young readers.

Emerging Readers
(no flags)

Beginning Readers
(1 flag)

Transitional Readers
(2 flags)

Fluent Readers
(3 flags)

These levels are meant only as a guide. All levels are subject to change.

FACT & Fiction

This series provides early fluent readers the opportunity to develop reading comprehension strategies and increase fluency. These books are appropriate for guided, shared, and independent reading.

FACT The left-hand pages incorporate realistic photographs to enhance readers' understanding of informational text.

Fiction The right-hand pages engage readers with an entertaining, narrative story that is supported by whimsical illustrations.

The Fact and Fiction pages can be read separately to improve comprehension through questioning, predicting, making inferences, and summarizing. They can also be read side-by-side, in spreads, which encourages students to explore and examine different writing styles.

FACT OR Fiction? This fun quiz helps reinforce students' understanding of what is real and not real.

SPEED READ The text-only version of each section includes word-count rulers for fluency practice and assessment.

GLOSSARY Higher-level vocabulary and concepts are defined in the glossary.

SandCastle™ would like to hear from you.

Tell us your stories about reading this book. What was your favorite page? Was there something hard that you needed help with? Share the ups and downs of learning to read. To get posted on the ABDO Publishing Company Web site, send us an e-mail at:

sandcastle@abdopublishing.com

Pigs are in the swine family. Male pigs are called boars, female pigs are called sows, and babies are called piglets.

Riblet Swine is a very happy piglet. He lives with his brothers, sister, mama, and papa in beautiful Wallow Lake Valley.

BIRD

SWINE

POOCH

5

Pigs are mammals and are very smart. The only mammals smarter than pigs are humans, primates, whales, and dolphins.

Riblet proudly thinks that his family is the smartest around! Mama is a teacher and Papa is a pilot. Hogsley loves math, Oink is a science whiz, and history is hog-heaven for Sooey.

Pigs can get bored. To keep from getting bored, pigs play with toys and stay active.

Riblet loves running as much as reading. Every day after doing his homework, Riblet races his littermates in the park. They are training for the Wallow School Fun Run.

Pigs only eat until they are full. Pigs mostly consume grains, grasses, and plants. They will also eat insects, worms, and small animals such as mice.

On the day of the run, there is a picnic before the race. Riblet nibbles watermelon and dreams of winning. "Don't pig out," he warns his brothers and sister. "It will slow us down!"

11

A pig's snout helps it find food. Pigs use their snouts to root for bugs and grubs to eat.

Hogsley roots in the picnic basket
for fruit salad. "Yum!" he squeals
when he finds it. The piglets eat just
enough. Next they admire the Fun
Run prize. It is a golden pig pen,
perfect for doing A+ schoolwork.

13

Pigs do not have sweat glands, so they roll in the mud to stay cool. The caked-on mud also protects their skin from insect bites.

Suddenly Sooey whispers, "Let's roll in the mud to keep cool!"

"Great idea!" Oink says. They hurry to the lakeside and wallow like wild boars. They trot back just in time to line up.

15

Pigs are fast. They can run a mile in seven minutes!

The starter calls, "Ready, set, go!" The racers take off. Riblet runs harder than he has ever run before. Mama and Papa cheer for their piglets.

GO!

HOGS RULE!

PIGS!

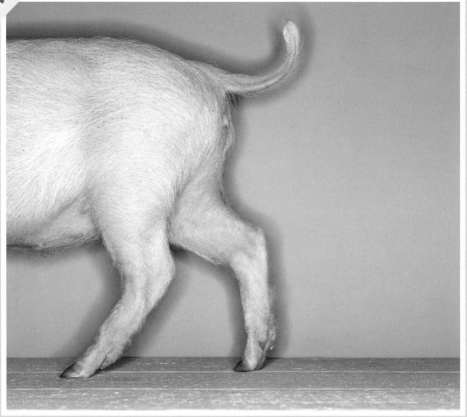

Pigs walk on only two of the four toes on each hoof. It looks like they are walking on tiptoe!

Riblet takes the lead. But as he nears the finish line, Hogsley, Sooey, and Oink catch up. The referee says, "It's a four-way tie. Golden pig pens for you all!" With a snort, Riblet breaks into a hip-hog dance. His happy littermates join in.

FACT OR Fiction?

Read each statement below. Then decide whether it's from the FACT section or the Fiction section!

  1. Female pigs are called sows.

  2. Pigs use pens to do schoolwork.

  3. Pigs read about history.

  4. Pigs walk on only two of the four toes on each hoof.

Pigs are in the swine family. Male pigs are called boars, female pigs are called sows, and babies are called piglets.

Pigs are mammals and are very smart. The only mammals smarter than pigs are humans, primates, whales, and dolphins.

Pigs can get bored. To keep from getting bored, pigs play with toys and stay active.

Pigs only eat until they are full. Pigs mostly consume grains, grasses, and plants. They will also eat insects, worms, and small animals such as mice.

A pig's snout helps it find food. Pigs use their snouts to root for bugs and grubs to eat.

Pigs do not have sweat glands, so they roll in the mud to stay cool. The caked-on mud also protects their skin from insect bites.

Pigs are fast. They can run a mile in seven minutes!

Pigs walk on only two of the four toes on each hoof. It looks like they are walking on tiptoe!

10
19
21
30
37
40
49
56
65
74
82
93
101
112
122
127
138
150
158

Riblet Swine is a very happy piglet. He lives 9
with his brothers, sister, mama, and papa in 17
beautiful Wallow Lake Valley. 21

Riblet proudly thinks that his family is the 29
smartest around! Mama is a teacher and Papa is 38
a pilot. Hogsley loves math, Oink is a science 47
whiz, and history is hog-heaven for Sooey. 55

Riblet loves running as much as reading. 62
Every day after doing his homework, Riblet races 70
his littermates in the park. They are training for 79
the Wallow School Fun Run. 84

On the day of the run, there is a picnic before 95
the race. Riblet nibbles watermelon and dreams 102
of winning. "Don't pig out," he warns his 110
brothers and sister. "It will slow us down!" 118

Hogsley roots in the picnic basket for fruit 126
salad. "Yum!" he squeals when he finds it. The 135
piglets eat just enough. Next they admire the 143

22

Fun Run prize. It is a golden pig pen, perfect for 154
doing A+ schoolwork. 157

Suddenly Sooey whispers, "Let's roll in the mud 165
to keep cool!" 168

"Great idea!" Oink says. They hurry to the 176
lakeside and wallow like wild boars. They trot back 185
just in time to line up. 191

The starter calls, "Ready, set, go!" The racers take 200
off. Riblet runs harder than he has ever run before. 210
Mama and Papa cheer for their piglets. 217

Riblet takes the lead. But as he nears the finish 227
line, Hogsley, Sooey, and Oink catch up. The referee 236
says, "It's a four-way tie. Golden pig pens for you 247
all!" With a snort, Riblet breaks into a hip-hog 257
dance. His happy littermates join in. 263

GLOSSARY

admire. to regard with pleasure, wonder, and approval

grub. a thick, wormlike insect larva

mammal. a warm-blooded vertebrate that is covered in hair and, in the female, produces milk to feed the young

root. 1) to dig in the dirt with the snout 2) to search for something

snout. the projecting nose or jaws of an animal's head

squeal. to make a high-pitched cry or sound

wallow. to roll around in water, snow, or mud

To see a complete list of SandCastle™ books and other nonfiction titles from ABDO Publishing Company, visit www.abdopublishing.com or contact us at: 4940 Viking Drive, Edina, Minnesota 55435 • 1-800-800-1312 • fax: 1-952-831-1632